YOUR COMPLETE CANCER 2025 PERSONAL HOROSCOPE

Monthly Astrological Prediction Forecast Readings of Every Zodiac Astrology Sun Star Signs- Love, Romance, Money, Finances, Career, Health, Travel, Spirituality.

Iris Quinn

Alpha Zuriel Publishing

Your Complete Cancer 2025 Personal Horoscope/ Iris Quinn. -- 1st ed.

"Astrology is a language. If you understand this language, the sky speaks to you."
— IRIS QUINN

CONTENTS

CHAPTER ONE

CANCER PROFILE

General Characteristics

- **Element:** Water
- **Quality:** Cardinal
- **Ruler:** Moon
- **Symbol:** The Crab
- **Dates:** June 21 - July 22

Personality Traits

- **Nurturing:** Naturally caring and protective.
- **Emotional:** Deeply in touch with their feelings and those of others.
- **Intuitive:** Strong instinct and ability to sense what others need.
- **Loyal:** Devoted and committed to loved ones.
- **Compassionate:** Empathetic and understanding.
- **Protective:** Takes care of loved ones and shields them from harm.
- **Sensitive:** Easily affected by the emotions and actions of others.

- **Creative:** Imaginative and artistic.
- **Moody:** Can experience frequent emotional ups and downs.
- **Cautious:** Tends to be careful and considerate before taking action.

Strengths

- **Empathy:** Great at understanding and sharing the feelings of others.
- **Loyalty:** Highly faithful and devoted to family and friends.
- **Nurturing:** Excellent caregivers and supporters.
- **Intuition:** Strong instinctual awareness and understanding of people.
- **Creativity:** Highly imaginative and artistic.
- **Resilience:** Able to recover from setbacks with inner strength.

Weaknesses

- **Moodiness:** Prone to frequent changes in mood.
- **Sensitivity:** Can be easily hurt by criticism or harsh words.
- **Insecurity:** May doubt themselves and seek reassurance from others.
- **Clinginess:** Can become overly attached to loved ones.
- **Cautiousness:** Sometimes overly wary and hesitant to take risks.
- **Defensiveness:** Can be protective to the point of being defensive.

Planets and Their Influences

- **Career Planet:** Saturn – Provides discipline and a strong work ethic in professional life.
- **Love Planet:** Venus – Governs love, beauty, and romantic relationships.
- **Money Planet:** Moon – Influences financial intuition and emotional spending habits.
- **Planet of Fun, Entertainment, Creativity, and Speculations:** Jupiter – Encourages joy and creativity.
- **Planet of Health and Work:** Mercury – Influences routine, health, and communication.
- **Planet of Home and Family Life:** Moon – Governs emotions, instincts, and domestic affairs.
- **Planet of Spirituality:** Neptune – Represents dreams, intuition, and spiritual pursuits.
- **Planet of Travel, Education, Religion, and Philosophy:** Jupiter – Governs growth, learning, and philosophical outlooks.

Compatibility

- **Signs of Greatest Overall Compatibility:** Scorpio, Pisces
- **Signs of Greatest Overall Incompatibility:** Aries, Libra
- **Sign Most Supportive for Career Advancement:** Capricorn
- **Sign Most Supportive for Emotional Well-being:** Taurus
- **Sign Most Supportive Financially:** Virgo

- **Sign Best for Marriage and/or Partnerships:** Scorpio
- **Sign Most Supportive for Creative Projects:** Pisces
- **Best Sign to Have Fun With:** Sagittarius
- **Signs Most Supportive in Spiritual Matters:** Pisces
- **Best Day of the Week:** Monday

Additional Details

- **Colors:** Silver, White
- **Gem:** Pearl
- **Scent:** Jasmine, Gardenia
- **Birthstone:** Ruby
- **Quality:** Cardinal (initiates and leads)

PERSONALITY OF CANCER

Cancer, born between June 21 and July 22, is a water sign ruled by the Moon, which deeply influences their personality with traits of nurturing, sensitivity, and intuition. Individuals born under this sign are known for their caring nature and their ability to connect emotionally with others. They have a strong desire to nurture and protect those they love, often taking on the role of the caregiver in their relationships.

At the core of a Cancer's personality is their emotional depth. They feel things profoundly and have a remarkable ability to understand and empathize with the emotions of others. This emotional intelligence allows them to offer comfort and support to those around them, making them cherished friends and partners. Their intuition is another key aspect of their character, often giving them a keen sense of what others are feeling or thinking, even without words.

Cancers are fiercely loyal and dedicated to their loved ones. They form strong bonds and are always willing to go the extra mile to ensure the happiness and well-being of those they care about. This loyalty is unwavering, and once they commit to someone, they remain steadfast and true. Their sense of loyalty also extends to their home and family, which they hold in the highest regard. Home is a sanctuary for Cancer, a place where they can retreat and feel safe. They invest a lot of energy in creating a warm and inviting home environment, often finding joy in domestic activities and family gatherings.

Creativity is another prominent trait of Cancer individuals. They have a vivid imagination and a natural flair for the arts, whether it be music, painting, writing, or other forms of creative expression. This creativity often serves as an emotional outlet for them, helping them process their deep feelings and share their inner world with others. Their artistic talents are often intertwined with their sensitivity, allowing them to create works that resonate emotionally with others.

However, the sensitivity of Cancer can also be a double-edged sword. While it enables them to connect deeply with others, it also makes them prone to mood swings and emotional fluctuations. They can be easily hurt by criticism or harsh words, and they tend to take things personally. This emotional vulnerability requires them to seek environments and relationships that are nurturing and supportive.

Cancers are also known for their cautious nature. They are not quick to take risks and prefer to move through life with careful consideration. This cautiousness is driven by their need for security and stability. They seek to create a safe and predictable environment for themselves and their loved ones, often avoiding situations that could lead to uncertainty or danger.

Despite their cautious approach, Cancers possess a resilient spirit. They have an innate ability to bounce back from setbacks and challenges. This resilience is rooted in their deep emotional strength and their unwavering commitment to their goals and loved ones. When faced with adversity, they draw on their inner reserves of strength and emerge even stronger.

In relationships, Cancers are deeply loving and devoted partners. They value emotional connection and seek a partner who can understand and appreciate their sensitive nature. They are generous with their affection and are always looking for ways to show their love and care. However, they also need a partner who can provide reassurance and emotional stability, as they can sometimes struggle with insecurity and self-doubt.

Cancers are complex individuals with a rich emotional landscape. Their nurturing and empathetic nature makes them invaluable friends and partners, while their creativity and intuition add depth and richness to their personality. Though they may face challenges due to their sensitivity and cautiousness, their resilience and loyalty help them navigate life with grace and strength. Those who take the time to understand and appreciate a Cancer's unique qualities will find a deeply loving and devoted companion who enriches their life in countless ways.

WEAKNESSES OF CANCER

Cancer, while possessing many admirable qualities, also has weaknesses that can present challenges in their personal and professional lives. One of the most notable weaknesses of Cancer is their sensitivity. They are deeply emotional beings, and this heightened sensitivity means they can be easily hurt by the actions and words of others. Even minor criticisms or perceived slights can wound them deeply, leading to feelings of insecurity and self-doubt. This sensitivity often causes them to retreat into their shell, much like their symbol, the Crab, when they feel threatened or vulnerable.

Another significant weakness of Cancer is their tendency towards moodiness. Their emotions can fluctuate rapidly, influenced by both internal feelings and external circumstances. This moodiness can make them unpredictable, and those around them may find it challenging to navigate their changing emotional states. Cancers themselves often struggle with these shifts, finding it difficult to maintain emotional equilibrium.

Cancers are also prone to being overly cautious. Their need for security and stability can make them reluctant to take risks or step out of their comfort zone. This cautiousness, while sometimes beneficial, can hold them back from seizing opportunities and experiencing new things. They may miss out on personal and professional growth because of their fear of the unknown or potential failure.

In relationships, Cancers can be overly protective and clingy. Their deep care and concern for their loved ones can sometimes become overwhelming, leading them to smother those they care about. This overprotectiveness can stifle the independence of their partners and create tension. Additionally, their fear of losing those they love can make them possessive, leading to jealousy and insecurity in their relationships.

Cancers also tend to hold onto the past. They have a strong connection to their memories and can find it difficult to let go of past hurts and disappointments. This attachment to the past can prevent them from fully moving forward and embracing new experiences. They might dwell on old grievances, which can create a barrier to personal growth and the development of healthy relationships.

Another challenge for Cancer is their tendency to internalize their emotions. They often keep their true feelings hidden, preferring to deal with their issues privately rather than sharing them with others. This can lead to a buildup of unresolved emotions and stress. Over time, this internalization can manifest as anxiety, depression, or physical health issues. It's important for Cancer to learn to open up and express their emotions in a healthy way, seeking support when needed.

Cancers can also be overly nurturing to the point of neglecting their own needs. Their selfless nature drives them to take care of others, sometimes at their own expense. They may struggle to set boundaries and say no, leading to feelings of being overwhelmed or taken for granted. This excessive nurturing can drain their energy and leave them feeling depleted, both emotionally and physically.

Finally, Cancer's tendency to be pessimistic can be a significant weakness. Their fear of the unknown and potential failure can lead them to expect the worst in situations. This pessimism can affect their outlook on life, making it difficult for them to stay positive and hopeful. It's essential for Cancer to cultivate a more balanced perspective and focus on the positive aspects of their experiences.

In conclusion, while Cancer's sensitivity, emotional depth, and nurturing nature are among their greatest strengths, these same traits can also be sources of weakness. Their sensitivity can lead to hurt feelings and insecurity, their moodiness can create unpredictability, and their cautiousness can hold them back from growth and new experiences. Overprotectiveness and an attachment to the past can strain their relationships, while internalizing emotions can lead to stress and health issues. By recognizing and addressing these weaknesses, Cancer can work towards achieving greater balance and emotional well-being, allowing their positive qualities to shine even brighter.

RELATIONSHIP COMPATIBILITY WITH CANCER

Based only on their Sun signs, this is how Cancer interacts with others. These are the compatibility interpretations for all 12 potential Cancer combinations. This is a limited and insufficient method of determining compatibility.

However, Sun-sign compatibility remains the foundation for overall harmony in a relationship.

The general rule is that yin and yang do not get along. Yin complements yin, and yang complements yang. While yin and yang partnerships can be successful, they require more effort. Earth and water zodiac signs are both Yin. Yang is represented by the fire and air zodiac signs.

Cancer with Yin Signs (Earth and Water)

Cancer and Taurus (Yin with Yin):

Cancer and Taurus share a natural affinity, as both signs value security, stability, and a comfortable home life. Cancer's nurturing nature complements Taurus' practicality and reliability, creating a harmonious and supportive relationship. Taurus appreciates Cancer's emotional depth and care, while Cancer admires Taurus' steadfastness and dedication. They both enjoy creating a warm and inviting home, filled with love and mutual respect. Their biggest challenge may be Taurus' occasional stubbornness clashing with Cancer's sensitivity. However, their mutual commitment to building a solid foundation helps them overcome any minor conflicts, resulting in a deeply satisfying and enduring partnership.

Cancer and Virgo (Yin with Yin):

Cancer and Virgo form a nurturing and practical duo, with each sign bringing complementary strengths to the relationship. Virgo's attention to detail and methodical approach to life balance Cancer's emotional depth and intuitive nature. Virgo provides the stability and organization that Cancer craves, while Cancer offers warmth and emotional support that helps Virgo feel appreciated. Their shared values of loyalty and dedication strengthen their bond, making them a strong and supportive team. The main challenge lies in Virgo's critical nature, which can sometimes hurt Cancer's sensitive feelings. Effective communication and mutual understanding are key to maintaining harmony in this relationship.

Cancer and Capricorn (Yin with Yin):

Cancer and Capricorn are opposite signs that complement each other well. Cancer's nurturing and empathetic nature balances Capricorn's ambition and practicality. Capricorn provides the security and stability that Cancer desires, while Cancer offers emotional depth and care that helps Capricorn feel loved and supported. Their relationship thrives on mutual respect and a shared commitment to building a solid future. However, Cancer's emotional approach can sometimes clash with Capricorn's more reserved and pragmatic demeanor. Patience and understanding are essential for bridging this gap and creating a harmonious and fulfilling partnership.

Cancer and Scorpio (Yin with Yin):

Cancer and Scorpio share a deep emotional connection, making their relationship intense and passionate. Both signs value loyalty, intimacy, and emotional depth, creating a bond that is both powerful and transformative. Cancer's nurturing nature complements Scorpio's intensity, and together they form a protective and supportive partnership. Scorpio appreciates Cancer's care and sensitivity, while Cancer admires Scorpio's strength and determination. Their biggest challenge may be managing their strong emotions and occasional bouts of jealousy. Open communication and mutual trust are crucial for maintaining balance and harmony in this deeply passionate relationship.

Cancer and Pisces (Yin with Yin):

Cancer and Pisces are a highly compatible pair, sharing a profound emotional and intuitive connection. Both signs are sensitive, compassionate, and value emotional intimacy, creating a nurturing and harmonious relationship. Cancer's protective and caring nature resonates with Pisces' need for understanding and emotional support. Pisces' creativity and dreaminess bring a sense of magic and inspiration to Cancer's life. They understand each other's needs and are willing to go to great lengths to ensure each other's happiness. Their main challenge may be their mutual tendency towards emotional vulnerability. However, their deep empathy and mutual support help them navigate any difficulties, resulting in a loving and fulfilling partnership.

Cancer with Yang Signs (Fire and Air)

Cancer and Aries (Yin with Yang):

Cancer and Aries have contrasting energies that can make their relationship challenging but potentially rewarding. Aries' dynamic and assertive nature contrasts with Cancer's nurturing and sensitive disposition. Aries can bring excitement and a sense of adventure to Cancer's life, encouraging them to step out of their comfort zone. Conversely, Cancer can offer emotional support and care, helping Aries to slow down and appreciate the more subtle aspects of life. Their biggest challenge is Aries' impulsiveness and directness, which can sometimes hurt Cancer's delicate feelings. Patience, compromise, and mutual respect are essential for making this relationship work.

Cancer and Leo (Yin with Yang):

Cancer and Leo have a relationship that combines warmth and loyalty with emotional depth and creativity. Leo's charisma and confidence blend well with Cancer's nurturing and empathetic nature, creating a dynamic and supportive partnership. Cancer admires Leo's strength and generosity, while Leo appreciates Cancer's care and devotion. However, Leo's need for attention and admiration can sometimes clash with Cancer's desire for emotional security and reassurance. Communication and mutual understanding are key to maintaining balance and harmony in this relationship, allowing both partners to feel valued and loved.

Cancer and Sagittarius (Yin with Yang):

Cancer and Sagittarius have very different approaches to life, which can create both challenges and opportunities for growth. Sagittarius' adventurous and free-spirited nature contrasts with Cancer's need for security and stability. Sagittarius can introduce excitement and new perspectives to Cancer's life, encouraging them to be more open and adventurous. Conversely, Cancer can offer emotional depth and stability, helping Sagittarius feel more grounded. Their biggest challenge is balancing Sagittarius' need for freedom with Cancer's desire for closeness and emotional connection. Patience, compromise, and clear communication are essential for making this relationship work.

Cancer and Gemini (Yin with Yang):

Cancer and Gemini have contrasting energies that can make their relationship both challenging and enriching. Gemini's intellectual and communicative nature contrasts with Cancer's emotional and intuitive approach to life. Gemini can bring variety and mental stimulation to Cancer's life, while Cancer offers emotional depth and care that helps Gemini feel more connected. However, Gemini's inconsistency and need for variety can sometimes clash with Cancer's desire for stability and reassurance. Mutual understanding, patience, and a willingness to adapt to each other's needs are crucial for maintaining a harmonious and fulfilling relationship.

Cancer and Libra (Yin with Yang):

Cancer and Libra create a partnership that combines emotional depth with a love for harmony and beauty. Libra's charm, diplomacy, and social nature complement Cancer's nurturing and empathetic disposition. Cancer admires Libra's ability to create balance and harmony, while Libra appreciates Cancer's care and emotional support. Their biggest challenge is managing Libra's indecisiveness and need for social interaction, which can sometimes clash with

Cancer's desire for emotional security and privacy. Effective communication and mutual respect are essential for maintaining harmony and balance in this relationship, allowing both partners to feel valued and understood.

Cancer and Aquarius (Yin with Yang):

Cancer and Aquarius have very different energies, which can create both challenges and opportunities for growth. Aquarius' innovative and independent nature contrasts with Cancer's need for emotional connection and security. Aquarius can introduce new ideas and perspectives to Cancer's life, encouraging them to be more open-minded and adventurous. Conversely, Cancer offers emotional depth and care that helps Aquarius feel more connected. Their biggest challenge is balancing Aquarius' need for freedom and independence with Cancer's desire for closeness and emotional intimacy. Patience, understanding, and a willingness to adapt to each other's needs are crucial for making this relationship work.

In conclusion, Cancer's compatibility with other sun signs varies widely based on the yin and yang theory. Earth and water signs generally complement Cancer's nurturing and empathetic nature, leading to harmonious and supportive relationships. Fire and air signs, while presenting more challenges, can provide excitement and growth, requiring more effort to navigate their differences. With mutual respect, understanding, and a willingness to learn from each other, Cancer can form successful and fulfilling partnerships with any sign.

LOVE AND PASSION

Love and passion for Cancer are deeply intertwined with their emotional and intuitive nature. As a water sign ruled by the Moon, Cancer individuals approach love with a profound sensitivity and a nurturing spirit. They are known for their capacity to form deep, emotional bonds with their partners, seeking relationships that offer both emotional intimacy and security. For Cancer, love is not just a feeling but a profound connection that encompasses both heart and soul.

When Cancer falls in love, they do so with their entire being. They are incredibly devoted and loyal, placing their partner's happiness and well-being above their own. This selfless approach to love stems from their inherent need to nurture and care for those they hold dear. A Cancer in love will go to great lengths to create a safe and comfortable environment for their partner, ensuring that they feel cherished and supported. This nurturing nature makes them exceptionally attentive and considerate lovers, always attuned to their partner's needs and emotions.

Cancer's passion is expressed through their deep emotional connections and their ability to empathize with their partner's feelings. They have an uncanny ability to sense what their partner needs, often without a word being spoken. This intuitive understanding allows them to provide comfort and reassurance, making their partner feel truly seen and understood. Cancer's passion is not always loud and fiery but rather a steady and constant flame that warms and nurtures over time.

In a relationship, Cancer seeks a partner who can match their emotional depth and provide the same level of commitment and loyalty. They crave a bond that goes beyond the physical, yearning for a connection that touches the soul. For Cancer, true passion is found in the small, everyday moments of intimacy and connection. They find great joy in simple acts of love, such as holding hands, sharing a quiet meal, or just being present with their partner. These moments of togetherness are what fuel their passion and keep the flame of love burning brightly.

However, Cancer's deep sensitivity can also be a source of vulnerability in love. They can be easily hurt by careless words or actions, and their tendency to take things personally can lead to feelings of insecurity.

This vulnerability means that Cancer needs a partner who is gentle, understanding, and capable of providing the emotional reassurance they crave. When they feel safe and loved, Cancer's passion can blossom fully, creating a relationship that is rich in emotional depth and mutual understanding.

Cancer's love life is also deeply influenced by their connection to home and family. They often view their partner as an integral part of their inner circle, and they take great pride in creating a loving and nurturing home environment. This connection to home life means that they value stability and long-term commitment, often seeking a partner who shares their desire for a family and a secure future together. Their passion for creating a harmonious and loving home extends to their relationship, where they strive to build a foundation of trust and mutual respect.

In moments of conflict, Cancer's emotional nature can sometimes lead to intense reactions. They may retreat into their shell when hurt or upset, needing time to process their emotions before they can communicate effectively. It is important for their partner to be patient and give them the space they need to feel safe enough to open up. Once Cancer feels understood and valued, their passion and love can flourish, bringing a profound sense of connection and intimacy to the relationship.

Cancer's passion is also expressed through their creativity and imagination. They often bring a touch of romance and magic to their relationships, surprising their partner with thoughtful gestures and heartfelt expressions of love. Whether through writing a heartfelt letter, preparing a favorite meal, or planning a special date, Cancer's creative expressions of love are always deeply personal and meaningful.

Ultimately, love and passion for Cancer are about creating a deep, emotional connection that provides security, understanding, and mutual devotion. They are deeply caring and intuitive lovers who seek a partner capable of matching their emotional depth and commitment. With the right partner, Cancer's love is a nurturing and transformative force, creating a relationship that is both deeply fulfilling and enduring.

MARRIAGE

Marriage for Cancer is a profound journey rooted in deep emotional connections, loyalty, and a strong desire for security and stability. Governed by the Moon, Cancer individuals bring a nurturing and protective energy to their marital relationships, seeking to create a sanctuary where love and mutual support thrive. To keep a Cancer happy in marriage, it is essential to understand their need for emotional closeness and a secure home environment. They value partners who are attentive to their feelings, who communicate openly, and who are committed to building a lasting bond based on trust and mutual respect.

Cancer men in marriage are deeply devoted and protective. They view their role as a husband with a sense of responsibility, often striving to provide and care for their family in every possible way. A Cancer man is typically affectionate and loving, valuing the small, daily acts of kindness that strengthen the marital bond. He seeks a partner who appreciates his nurturing nature and who is willing to reciprocate his deep emotional investment. To keep a Cancer man happy in marriage, it is crucial to show appreciation for his efforts and to create an emotionally warm and supportive home environment. Encouraging him to express his feelings and providing reassurance when needed helps him feel secure and valued.

Cancer women in marriage bring a similar nurturing and protective spirit. They are often the heart of the home, ensuring that everyone feels loved and cared for. A Cancer woman values emotional intimacy and seeks a partner who can share in her desire to create a loving and harmonious household. She is deeply empathetic and intuitive, often sensing her partner's needs before they are voiced. To keep a Cancer woman happy in marriage, it is important to show her consistent love and affection, to communicate openly, and to support her emotional needs. She thrives in an environment where she feels cherished and understood, where her efforts to nurture and care are recognized and appreciated.

The secret to making a marriage with Cancer work lies in understanding and respecting their emotional depth and need for security. Cancer individuals are highly sensitive and can be easily hurt by criticism or neglect. It is essential to create a safe space where they feel comfortable expressing their feelings and where open, honest communication is encouraged. Emotional reassurance and consistent expressions of love help to build a strong foundation of trust and intimacy.

One of the keys to a successful marriage with Cancer is to appreciate the importance they place on home and family. They often view their partner and family as the center of their world and invest a great deal of energy in creating a nurturing home environment. Supporting their efforts in this regard and sharing in the responsibilities of maintaining a happy household can strengthen the marital bond. Participating in family traditions, celebrating milestones, and creating lasting memories together help to reinforce the sense of unity and security that Cancer cherishes.

Another important aspect of maintaining a happy marriage with Cancer is to be patient and understanding of their mood swings. Cancer's emotions can fluctuate with the phases of the Moon, leading to periods of introspection or emotional intensity. During these times, it is crucial to offer support and understanding, allowing them the space to process their feelings. Showing empathy and patience helps to alleviate their insecurities and reinforces the emotional bond.

In moments of conflict, it is important to approach Cancer with sensitivity and care. Harsh words or aggressive behavior can deeply wound their sensitive nature. Constructive communication, where feelings are expressed calmly and respectfully, is vital. Demonstrating a willingness to listen and understand their perspective can help to resolve conflicts and strengthen the relationship. Forgiveness and the ability to move past disagreements with love and understanding are essential for maintaining harmony.

Cancer individuals also thrive on routines and rituals that provide a sense of stability and predictability. Establishing shared activities, such as regular date nights, family dinners, or weekend getaways, helps to create a sense of continuity and togetherness. These routines reinforce their need for security and demonstrate a shared commitment to nurturing the relationship.

In conclusion, marriage with Cancer is a deeply enriching experience that revolves around emotional connection, loyalty, and a shared commitment to building a secure and loving home. By understanding and honoring their need for emotional intimacy, providing consistent love and reassurance, and participating in the creation of a nurturing home environment, one can create a fulfilling and lasting marital bond with Cancer. Their nurturing and protective nature makes them dedicated and loving partners who bring warmth, empathy, and a deep sense of commitment to their marriages. With mutual respect, open communication, and a shared vision for the future, a marriage with Cancer can be a deeply satisfying and enduring partnership.

CHAPTER TWO

CANCER 2025 HOROSCOPE

Overview Cancer 2025

(June 21 - July 22)

Welcome, dear Cancers, to an astrological year that promises to be a profound journey of spiritual awakening, emotional healing, and a deepening connection to your innermost truths. As the celestial bodies dance their cosmic rhythms, they will illuminate both challenges and opportunities that will shape your evolution toward greater authenticity, inner peace, and soul-aligned manifestation. Prepare to dive deep into the depths of your psyche and shed the layers that have been obscuring your radiant essence.

The year begins with Mars transiting through the mystical waters of Pisces, amplifying your sensitivities and drawing you inward to explore your subconscious realms. This emerges as a fertile time for engaging with spiritual practices, artistic expression, or anything that facilitates a deeper attunement with your intuitive wisdom. Embrace solitude, ritual, and trust the signs and symbols that arise from your dreams and imagination.

A pivotal shift occurs on January 11th when the karmic North Node ingresses into Pisces, orchestrating an 18-month cycle centered on your spiritual unfoldment. This transit presents a powerful invitation to release any limiting beliefs, ancestral patterns or past life imprints that have disconnected you from your soul's essential nature. Modalities like past life regression, shamanic journeying or creative visualization could aid in integrating soul fragments. Stay open to profound awakenings.

On March 1st, stern taskmaster Saturn enters Aries, amplifying your 10th house of public image, career mastery and life's purpose. For the next few months until May, you'll face tests that require increased discipline, focus and confronting fears/limitations around visibility and authority. Any lingering insecurities or impostor complexes will get triggered to be healed. Trust that these hurdles are helping build the resilience and gravitas needed to fully step onto your soul's stage.

The Aries New Moon on March 29th, electrified by a Partial Solar Eclipse, provides rocket fuel for pivotal new beginnings in your professional and public realms. But with pragmatic Saturn's influence, your efforts must be grounded in sustainable strategies and diligent commitments. This eclipse marks the emergence of a new you that is ready to lead, be seen and share your authentic gifts fearlessly with the world.

In mid-April, expansive Jupiter's challenging square to transformative Pluto illuminates potent psychological shadows and power dynamics needing to be reckoned with in your closest unions. Toxic patterns of control, repression or subconscious sabotage get exposed, catalyzing profound emotional renewal and liberation within your bonds. For some, this could initiate relationship endings if necessary for growth. For others, a soul-rebirthing recommitment. Stay open to the lessons and prepare to do the deeper work.

June brings an exhilarating but also potentially volatile energy as your ruling planet Mars barrels into your sign on the 17th, stoking your courage, passion and personal willpower for the first time in two years. While this transit amplifies your charisma and capacity for bold self-expression, it also increases propensity for conflicts, power struggles and reactive outbursts you'll need to temper. Channel this forceful fire sign energy into assertive goal-setting and courageous authenticity, but avoid burning bridges selfishly.

The Lunar Eclipse in Sagittarius on June 11th shines a spotlight on your 9th house of wisdom, growth experiences and worldly exploration. An awakening around your personal philosophies, belief structures or perspectives on "truth" could rock your world, setting you on an expanded trajectory to broaden your horizons through travel, cross-cultural immersion or higher learning. Be open to exploring new teachings and leaving your comfort zones. Unexpected journeys await!

The season of Cancer arrives on June 20th with the Solstice, kicking off your personal New Year energy! At this auspicious time, take stock of the profound shifts that have already occurred and set empowered intentions for the continued rebirth and reclamation of your sovereignty in the months ahead. The New Moon in your sign on June 26th provides cosmic fertile ground for these new beginnings, whether personal evolutions or launches of important initiatives.

July 16th brings sweet relief from the intense activations of the first half of the year as abundant Jupiter finally shifts into Cancer and your 4th house of home, family and emotional foundations. For the next 12 months, you'll experience expansive blessings in nurturing your deepest feelings of safety, belonging and inner contentment. This is a beautiful year for strengthening family bonds, creating your dream living space, and establishing roots that allow you to blossom into your most authentic self. Make your home a sanctuary.

The second half of 2025 requires your focus and determination as Saturn finally arrives at his destination in Aries and your 10th house of worldly domain. From August through 2028, you'll face an extended period of being tested around commitment to your ambitions and long-term goals. Structures and diligence will need to be constructed to support the public emergence and visibility your soul's work requires. Know that these challenges, while demanding, are ultimately fortifying your force of character as a respected master at the height of your craft or calling.

September brings more evolutionary shifts and reinventions as the Virgo New Moon on the 22nd arrives accompanied by a Partial Solar Eclipse in your 5th house of creativity, joy and self-expression. With catalytic Pluto involved, you may experience sudden awakenings or breakdowns around how you've been self-censoring your authenticity and playing it "safe" with sharing your full truth. This cosmic rebirthing sets you on a raw, courageous path of unapologetically creating from your heart's inspiration and no longer suppressing your passions for anyone's approval. Flow your art, speak your poetry, birth your unique creations without fear!

This theme of authenticity and celebrating your life force currents extends into your relationships as well, with passionate Mars entering your partnership sector on September 22nd. You may experience a rekindling of romantic sparks and creative collaborations that feel energizing and liberating. For some, this initiates new attractions that help you embody your sensual essence. However, watch for power dynamics or ego conflicts arising that require clear boundaries and vulnerability. Lead with the radiant heart you've reclaimed.

The year begins winding down in October with expansive Jupiter entering your communication sector on the 21st, blessing you with inspiration, optimism and new avenues for sharing your ideas/philosophies more widely. Higher learning curriculums, writing/media projects or publication endeavors get green-lit during this transit into mid-2026. Share your unique voice and watch your reach organically grow.

Anchor into your personal power, wisdom and emotional mastery as the astrological year concludes in December with a Capricorn New Moon Solar Eclipse in your 8th house of intimacy, shared resources and psycho-spiritual rebirth. This potent lunation shines a light on any remnant self-sabotaging patterns of disempowerment, lack mentality or limiting beliefs around your Divine deservingness of sovereignty. With Pluto involved, emotional catharsis unlocks profound awakenings and richer capacities for vulnerability and tantric merging—whether figuratively with the Beloved Self, or literally with others. Own your depth, radiance and multitudes, honorable Cancer. You've reclaimed your majesty.

This year, the planets are conspiring to purify you of layers of conditioning and programming that have obscured the magnitude of your luminous, feeling, psychically potent essence. While intense internal and external shake-ups will feel confronting at times, trust these are necessary initiations into a more authentic, self-actualized version of your soul's intentions. Embrace solitude when you need it, but know your sensitivity is also a source of profound strength to be shared with the world. Allow the currents of 2025 to awaken you to the depths of your being, so that from these cleansed roots, you can more radiantly embody and manifest your soul's wisdom out into sacred form. The journey inward ultimately births the beauty outward.

January 2025

Overview Horoscope for the Month:

As we ring in the new year, the celestial energies are beckoning you inward, dear Cancer. With a powerful lineup of planets traveling through the deep, transformative waters of Pisces, January 2025 emerges as a time for profound introspection, emotional release, and a return to your intuitive roots. While the external world may seem hushed, a rich inner awakening is stirring that will ultimately rebirth you with greater sensitivity and connection to your soul's truth. Prepare to go within and listen.

Love:

Your romantic partnerships take on an intense, soul-merging tone this January thanks to Venus and Mars transiting through Pisces and igniting your 8th house of intimacy and psychic bonding. Existing bonds will feel driven to explore deeper levels of erotic communion, emotional transparency, and shared vulnerability. For singles, attractions could feel fated or catalytic for core psychological work and profound awakenings. However, power dynamics or shadow projections in relationships may also get triggered now, requiring you to strengthen self-awareness. Lead with your heart's wisdom.

Career:

While your external career goals may not be the major focus this month, Cancer, January's cosmic energies are offering you opportunities to realign your professional path with greater authenticity and purpose. With taskmaster Saturn still trekking through your public sector until May, you'll continue being pushed to show up with maturity and personal authority. However, the Pisces planets are also illuminating blind spots or misalignments between your worldly ambitions and your innermost values. Get clear now on the "why" fueling your work to manifest increased soul-fulfillment moving forward.

Finances:

The Capricorn energies of the past few months brought a pragmatic focus on budgets, financial strategy, and building material security, dear Cancer. In January though, the celestial tides turn more toward assessing your ingrained beliefs, attachments, and shadows related to abundance, self-worth, and wealth consciousness. With transformative Pluto traveling with the Sun, this is an incredibly fertile period for doing the inner work to heal your relationship to money, releasing fears or limiting patterns that block greater prosperity. Trust this psycho-spiritual excavation process, however intense.

Health:

With outgoing Mars touring your restful 12th house this January, you'll likely be craving extended time and space to nurture your spiritual and emotional wellbeing. Take advantage of this cosmic pause by immersing yourself in restorative practices that soothe your sensitive soul - things like meditation, breathwork, artistic expression or spiritual studies. Nourish yourself with solitude, gentle bodywork, and honoring any feelings that need to be felt and released. As the first month of the year, this is a beautiful reset for your mental, physical and psychic self-care.

Travel:

With so much inward-turning, psychological energy swirling this month, international travel or worldly adventures feel less emphasized in January, dear Cancer. However, you may feel drawn to taking rejuvenating solo retreats or pilgrimages to sacred sites that replenish your spiritual wellspring. Locations near bodies of water could feel especially cathartic, as could any place that facilitates solitude, ritual, and deepening your mystical studies or connections. For now, look for inspiration closer to home before venturing afar later in 2025.

Insights from the Stars:

The key astrological forces illuminating your journey through January are all about diving inward to access the wisdom of your subconscious, dear Cancer. This is a potent period for psychological and spiritual rebirth where you'll be pushed to confront any shadows, attachments or fears that have disconnected you from your sensitivity and authentic self-expression. While this process could feel intense or disorienting at times, trust that it's divinely choreographed to purify you down to your truth. Embrace solitude and trust the signs from your dreams and visions. Tremendous growth lives in surrendering to your intuition.

Best Days:

- January 6th: Mars sextile Uranus - Seize this energy for assertion, innovation, and following your personal freedom!

- January 14th: Venus sextile Uranus - Your powers of attraction, joy and magnetism get amplified. Socialize!
- January 18th: Mercury conjunct Pluto - Fantastic for delving into psychological depths through research or conversations.
- January 23rd: New Moon in Aquarius - This group-oriented lunation provides fertile soil for social initiatives or original collaborations.
- January 30th: Uranus stations direct - Clarity and momentum returns after periods of reassessment. Stay open-minded..

February 2025

Overview Horoscope for the Month:

February brings a powerful convergence of planetary energies that will catalyze major shifts and transformations in your life, dear Cancer. The first half of the month is marked by a buildup of intensity, with Mars retrograding back into your sign on the 6th. This cosmic backspin will prompt you to revisit unfinished emotional business and reclaim your personal power. Simultaneously, revolutionary Uranus forms a potent alignment with the karmic North Node on the 7th, electrifying your spiritual axis. Profound awakenings are imminent!

The Full Moon Lunar Eclipse in Leo on the 12th is a game-changer. Monumental events surrounding relationships, creative expression, and your ability to shine could dramatically reshape your life's trajectory. Have courage and embrace the inevitable metamorphosis. The second half of February brings welcome relief as Mars turns direct on the 23rd, helping you reassert your drive. Anchor into your truth

as the New Moon in Pisces (27th) opens a fertile cycle
for planting intention seeds.

Love:

Your love life takes a radical turn this month as
dynamic forces conspire to obliterate stale relating
patterns. If coupled, Venus's lengthy journey through
fiery Aries could inflame passions deliciously or
problematically, depending on how consciously you
wield this potent erotic energy. Power struggles and
control issues may erupt, teaching you invaluable
lessons about balancing autonomy and intimacy. An
openness to transform your union is required.

For singles, this month's cosmic turbulence could
abruptly sever karmic ties, making room for a soul-
shaking connection. Be vigilant for someone who
magnetically draws you out of your defensive shell.
Just ensure you aren't being lured by an unhealthy
rescuer-fixer dynamic. Above all, February demands
you love yourself unconditionally through this molting
process.

Career:

The first three weeks of February are best reserved
for introspection regarding your professional
trajectory, rather than outward-directed ambition. With

Mars backspinning through your sign until the 23rd, you may struggle with waning motivation and self-doubt. Use this pause pragmatically to realign with your truest values and rework unsatisfying lifestyle patterns.

After Mars turns direct on the 23rd, you'll regain clarity and forward momentum. The potent Pisces New Moon (27th) opens an auspicious two-week period for planting seeds, be they job applications, business proposals, or creative projects expressing your talents. Have faith that the universe is conspiring to illuminate an authentic path aligned with your soul's purpose.

Finances:

Financial tensions could escalate to a breaking point in February, presenting you with radical choices to stabilize your economic foundation. An opportune Jupiter-Pluto alignment on the 17th brings the potential for a lucrative investment or strategy to increase prosperity. However, you may also be challenged to confront self-limiting attitudes impacting your abundance.

The Full Moon Lunar Eclipse (12th) could expose monetary vulnerabilities within a partnership that require you to rebalance the giving and receiving scales. Approaching issues of shared resources from a space of wisdom rather than fear will be a potent money magnet. As the month concludes, find inspired ways to monetize your passions and you'll attract abundance.

Health:

Take radical preventative self-care measures in February as this month's astrological intensity places considerable strain on your body's energetic reserves. With Mars retrograding through your sign until the 23rd, you'll need to consciously conserve vitality by resting deeply, staying hydrated, and simplifying your schedule. Meditative practices like yin yoga can counter excess cardinal fire and settle unrested minds.

The Pisces New Moon (27th) begins a fertile cycle for overhauling unhealthy lifestyle habits. Start a detoxifying cleanse, explore alternative therapies, or reduce your exposure to environmental toxins. Listen to your body's wisdom - it's communicating crucial messages about restoring equilibrium. Above all, treat yourself with infinite compassion as you shed old skins.

Travel:

Travel could figure prominently for you this month, whether literal or philosophical journeying. The Full Moon Eclipse on the 12th may open surprising gateways to venture abroad for personal or professional reasons, perhaps unexpectedly. Wherever you roam, step fully into the unfamiliar with a spirit of adventure.

For those staying closer to home, February's metamorphic energies make local exploration equally enriching. Wander alone in nature and study your reactions to the changing scenery. Be open to synchronicities illuminating your life's path. Above all, embrace an attitude of pilgrimage and sacred wonderment - the entire world is a classroom revealing vital lessons.

Insights from the Stars:

The cosmic skyscape in February imparts the wisdom that rebirth can only arise through the courageous release of all that no longer serves your highest evolution. You are being initiated into deeper self-mastery and spiritual authenticity, however disruptive or uncomfortable the metamorphic process may feel. Trust that you are being stripped of inessential baggage so your most brilliant light can shine forth unobstructed.

This is a prolific time for planting seeds, so visualize your soul's most cherished dreams with laser-focused intention. What you emanate now has incredible gestative power to bloom exponentially when properly nourished. Perhaps most importantly, remember you are never alone on this journey - unseen cosmic forces are offering protection, direction and abiding love.

Best Days of the Month:

- February 7th: Uranus conjoins the North Node, catalyzing lightning-bolt revelations and spiritual awakenings.
- February 12th: The Full Moon/Lunar Eclipse in Leo brings cathartic releases and dramatic plot twists in your life story. Surrender to the emotional depths.
- February 17th: A Jupiter-Pluto alignment brings opportunities for financial breakthroughs and increased prosperity.
- February 23rd: Mars turns direct in your sign after a lengthy retrograde, helping you regain confidence, courage and forward momentum.
- February 27th: The New Moon in Pisces opens a fertile new cycle for planting intentions and manifesting your inspired visions into reality.

March 2025

Overview Horoscope for the Month:

March opens up a cosmic gateway into new beginnings and fresh energy for you, Cancer. After an intense February, you'll feel a welcome reprieve as the Sun enters Aries on the 20th, kicking off the astrological new year in your relationship sector. This sparks a revival in your one-on-one connections and important partnerships. The New Moon in Aries on the 29th marks a powerful rebirth for how you relate. If coupled, renew your commitment to cooperation and compromise. If single, prepare for magnetic connections that reflect your evolving values.

Love:

Your love life undergoes a delicious reawakening this month as romantic potential fills the air. Venus, the planet of love, shifts into Aries on the 30th, activating passion and desire in your relationships. If involved, this cosmic honeymoon phase helps reignite the spark, but be mindful of old attachment patterns resurfacing. For singles, you'll feel an urge to merge coming on strong - just be discerning about who you choose to entangle with.

An exciting development arrives when lusty Mars enters Leo on the 18th, heating up your intimacy sector for the next six weeks. Creative expressions of affection and sexuality are favored now. Just watch for melodrama or power struggles that could accompany this fiery transit.

Career:

Your professional life is cosmically activated this month as the Aries New Moon on the 29th opens an auspicious new career cycle! The next two weeks are prime for launching enterprises, updating your resume/portfolio, or applying for new positions. Stay motivated, as opportunities are presenting themselves for you to make an impact.

However, with Mars transiting your privacy sector until the 18th, you may struggle with waning ambition or distractions on the home front. Save outward-directed efforts for after mid-month when you'll receive a welcome boost of energy for going after your goals with full force.

Finances:

Financial matters stabilize for you in March after any upheavals in February. An auspicious Jupiter-Chiron alignment on the 18th helps resolve monetary blocks or brings opportunities for increasing your prosperity. If debt has been weighing you down, this cosmic bonus helps you gain traction on a payment plan.

Stay attentive around the Full Moon on the 14th, which could expose vulnerabilities around shared resources that require renegotiation within a partnership. In general, this month is favorable for reviewing your cash flow and making thoughtful adjustments to build greater security.

Health:

With March's planets traveling through grounded earth signs, you'll be supported in establishing sustainable self-care routines this month. The first half finds potent Mars visiting your private sector, signaling your body requires extended rest and rejuvenation. Don't overtax your energy reserves now - schedule plenty of downtime.

As Mars moves into Leo mid-month, your vitality and motivation soar! Engage your creativity through dance, outdoor activities, or vibrant exercise that suits your current fitness level. The earthy Aries New Moon on the 29th is perfect for planting seeds like a new workout regimen or meal plan that supports your holistic well-being.

Travel:

March isn't the most auspicious month for taking extended journeys, with the planets focusing your gaze inward. However, the Full Moon in earthy Virgo on the 14th could bring an opportunity to visit nearby nature locales that help ground and recenter you. Solo hikes or beach strolls are favored now to reconnect with your elemental roots.

If traveling for business, the lunar eclipse on the 14th may unexpectedly require a work-related trip that ultimately expands your perspectives in positive ways. Just be sure to build in enough personal time to counterbalance heavy demands. An open mind and heart allows wisdom to flow from unexpected sources.

Insights from the Stars:

The star wisdom this month reminds you that your perspective creates your reality, beloved Cancer. As the feisty Aries energies pour into your relationships, remain mindful of where you're projecting old stories or limiting assumptions onto others. Choose to meet connections from a refreshed, receptive state and watch how dynamics beautifully transform and realign.

With six planets touring earthy Taurus and Virgo in March, you're also being encouraged to root more deeply into your body and surrounding environment. Replenish your spiritual and energetic stores by reverencing Mother Earth's tangible abundance. Savor nourishing flavors, sensual textures, euphonic sounds - open all your senses to receiving the divine generosity of nature's blessings.

Best Days of the Month:

- March 6th: First Quarter Moon in Gemini - Edifying discussions and short trips satisfy your curiosity.
- March 14th: Full Moon Lunar Eclipse in Virgo - A release around work or health, with positive developments despite any initial chaos.
- March 18th: Jupiter sextile Chiron - Lady Luck smiles upon you, helping you resolve financial/mindset blocks.
- March 20th: Sun enters Aries - A whole new personal cycle dawns, revitalizing you with fresh spirit!

- March 29th: New Moon in Aries - An auspicious window opens for planting seeds of intention in your relationships.

April 2025

Overview Horoscope for the Month:

April kicks off with potent cosmic energy activating your sectors of daily work, wellness routines, and small services to others. You'll be motivated to tackle any lingering tasks or chores around the home while also focusing on self-improvement. The New Moon in Aries on the 29th provides a fertile reboot for establishing productive habits and schedules. Just watch for moodiness or impatience during the first half of the month while fiery Mars travels through your privacy zone.

The fortunate trine between Jupiter and the karmic North Node on April 17th brings blessings through your social networks. Existing connections could lead to fortunate new opportunities blossoming. Prioritize circulating with those who inspire your highest vision. You're magnetic this month for attracting helpful people and fortuitous circumstances aligned with your soul's evolution.

Love:

April's planetary energy is largely focused on more pragmatic domestic and work matters rather than romance - but that doesn't mean your love life will be dull! In fact, this month provides some sweet surprises on the relationship front.

If coupled, the playful Aries New Moon (29th) helps reignite the fun, passion and laughter you first fell in love over. It's the perfect time for a spontaneous weekend getaway or any break from routine that allows you to reconnect as lovers. For singles, exciting introductions through friends, local networks or group activities are likely from mid-month onward once Mars fires up your social sector on the 18th. Be open to sparks flying when you least expect it!

Career:

Your work and life routines receive a cosmic reboot this April that allows you to hit refresh with increased energy, discipline and enthusiasm. The Aries New Moon in your six sector of habits on the 29th launches a fertile cycle for establishing better patterns around self-care, schedules and any job searching. With six planets touring earthy Taurus, you'll have abundant stamina and patience for making gradual, sustainable progress.

Expansion arrives around the 17th when the North Node aligns with expansive Jupiter. An opportunity to increase your income or launch an entrepreneurial venture may present itself during this auspicious window. Don't hesitate to showcase your skills and what you can offer prospective employers or clients. This month helps you assert your true worth in the workplace.

Finances:

Financial themes take a more positive turn this month after any February turbulence was cleared out by last month's eclipses. As disciplined Mars tours your resources sector until April 18th, you'll have increased motivation for budgeting, paying off debt, or carefully tracking where your money goes. This pragmatic cosmic helper can yield powerful results with a bit of strategy.

Once Mars fires up your income sector after the 18th, you could see new money-making opportunities developing, especially through social networking. The abundant North Node further amplifies your prosperity prospects, so continue showing up authentically and self-promoting your value. Positive returns are likely with concerted effort.

Health:

Make self-care routines a top priority this April
while the Sun, Mercury, Venus and the karmic lunar
nodes activate your wellness sector! You'll feel
potently inspired and motivated to adopt positive new
habits around diet, fitness, work-life balance or other
lifestyle adjustments that enhance your vitality. Don't
overcommit, but choose one achievable new regimen
to build into your schedule.

The New Moon on the 29th is fertile for beginning
a new program, treatment protocol, or different
approach to managing any chronic health conditions. If
the seeds you plant are nurtured consistently, you'll see
wonderful results ripening by late spring! Just don't
neglect sufficient rest and solitude time amidst all this
productive bustle.

Travel:

Travel isn't particularly highlighted for you this
month, Cancer darling. The planets are keeping your
gaze directed more inwardly towards local
surroundings and home atmospherics. However, the
Jupiter-North Node trine on the 17th could bring global
connections or mind-expanding exposures through
social circles and community networks.

If you do find yourself venturing farther afield,
you'll likely derive the most satisfaction from casual

day trips, solo sojourns or impromptu excursions with minimal advance planning. An open, spontaneous attitude allows you to make the most of unexpected encounters or chance discoveries during transit. No complex itineraries required - just remain effortlessly engaged with the world around you.

Insights from the Stars:

April's celestial wisdom encourages you to make yourself, your self-care routines and immediate environments top priority right now. The earthy Taurus emphasis gracing the skies says, "if you focus on creating solid foundations in all aspects of your daily existence, the rest will follow." When you establish life-enhancing daily patterns early in Spring's fertile cycle, greater ease and flow will naturally emerge as a result.

So take time to make your living spaces feel grounded and nurturing. Eat nourishing whole foods and notice how your energy increases. Trade mindless digital distractions for embodied activities that engage your senses. Get plenty of high-quality sleep too. These simple adjustments, however incremental they feel, can powerfully uplift your quality of life! Also watch for opportunities arriving through your circles near month's end - embrace what wants to grow through you.

Best Days of the Month:

- April 13th: Mars trines Pluto - You feel empowered pursuing your desires with unstoppable determination.
- April 17th: Jupiter trine North Node - An incredibly fortunate transit presenting golden opportunities via social connections.
- April 18th: Mars enters Virgo - Your energy and ambition receive a delicious reboot after waning in recent weeks. Excitingly productive times ahead!
- April 23rd: Sun enters Taurus - You're reinvigorated to establish a stable, prosperous and simple lifestyle amidst life's complexities. Grounded routines restore equilibrium.
- April 29th: New Moon in Aries - The perfect launchpad for making a fresh start with habits, self-care, work or wellness pursuits..

May 2025

Overview Horoscope for the Month:

May brings positive momentum and pragmatic progress after April's earthy restart, dear Cancer. The first half of the month is highly productive as motivating Mars tours your work and health sector. Coupled with abundant planetary energy in grounded Taurus, you'll feel inspired to improve routines, organize your environments, and establish sensible foundations. Just don't become overly rigid - leave room for spontaneity!

Relief and celebration arrive in the second half of May as the Sun enters lively Gemini on the 20th, kicking off your personal annual rebirth! The New Moon in Gemini on the 26th marks an especially fertile cycle for new beginnings linked to your self-expression, self-confidence and independence. Step into the spotlight and let your unique voice shine without apology.

Love:

Relationships take on a lighter, more fun-loving quality this month as amorous Venus ingresses into versatile Gemini on June 6th. If coupled, this sweet transit helps playfulness, laughter and easy communication flow more freely between you and your partner. Take a weekend trip together or find new ways to inject spontaneity into your shared routines.

For singles, exciting new flirtations and connections seem to spark out of nowhere once the Sun shifts into your sign on the 20th. Let your natural charisma and confidence shine and romance will be hard to avoid! Just be mindful of potential melodrama or mixed signals once messenger Mercury turns retrograde mid-June.

Career:

Work matters continue commanding center-stage in the first three weeks of May as dynamic Mars tours your sixth house of daily effort and organization. Your stamina and tolerance for detailed, meticulous tasks runs especially high during this cycle, so tackle any outstanding administrative duties or health checks. Just avoid being an overzealous perfectionist - some imperfections add character!

The arrival of the Gemini New Moon on the 26th brings a joyful creative rebirth that could unlock innovative ideas for earning additional income through your natural talents and communication skills. An Etsy store, boutique consulting services, or social media opportunities are just a few options to explore further. Let playfulness guide your moneymaking mindset right now.

Finances:

Financial streams should begin stabilizing this May as your planetary ruler, the Moon, forms supportive alignments with abundant Jupiter (18th) and Pluto (30th). If monetary tension or shortages have been creating anxiety, these transits provide much-needed breathing room, potentially through new income sources, debt restructuring or shedding financial drains.

The caveat is that Mercury, which oversees commerce and transactions, will turn retrograde from May 29th through June 22nd. During this signal scrambler, avoid major purchases or investments if possible and carefully review all documents before signing. Once the coast is clear in late June, you can revise budgets and payment plans with greater clarity.

Health:

Take full advantage of May's earthy, sensual Taurus vitality by engaging in physical activities that delight your senses. Time in nature hiking, cycling or tending a garden are favored for releasing any pent-up mental tensions stored in your body. The arrival of the Gemini New Moon cycle on the 25th also marks an ideal time for making sustainable dietary shifts or establishing new fitness goals - perhaps one focused on improved mobility and breathing?

If you've been managing chronic health issues, this is a great month for exploring complementary or alternative treatments. But avoid making any big changes or decisions until Mercury's retrograde clears in late June. For now, simply gather information and get in touch with your body's messaging without overthinking.

Travel:

Travel is looking fortuitous for you this May, Cancer! Especially around the Jupiter-Moon trine (18th) and expansive Gemini New Moon cycle kicking off on the 25th. These transits bring blessings toward fun adventures, wanderlust cravings and opportunities to experience new cultures, whether locally or abroad.

Solo road trips or overnight getaways are best when you can leave spontaneously without strict scheduling.

Trying something completely different from your regular routines - perhaps an immersive learning experience, retreat or cultural activity - helps you shift out of overthinking mode. The more open you can remain, the more synchronous magic moments will unfold!

Insights from the Stars:

The celestial insights this May remind you of the power in using your innate sensitivity as a sacred asset, rather than a burden. When you trust the messages your intuition and emotions are sending, infinite wisdom becomes available that the rational mind alone cannot access. This is your spiritual intelligence emerging, helping you navigate life's adventures with greater clarity and self-trust.

So breathe deeply, observe your feelings with neutral compassion, and allow yourself to experience the richness of every sense perception as it arises. The world reflects the beauty, wildness and mystery you can embrace within yourself. Shed what feels confining, and delight in embodying your unique self in joyful, playful ways. Rebirth is yours in May!

Best Days of the Month:

- May 2nd: Mars trine Pluto - You feel spiritually empowered and confident to follow your instincts.

- May 18th: Jupiter sextile Moon - Great good fortune arrives through networks, education, publishing or travel. An auspicious day for launches!

- May 20th: Sun enters Gemini - Your personal annual rebirth begins! The month ahead is filled with spontaneity, playfulness and reawakening.

- May 25th: Mars enters Leo - Your confidence, romantic desirability and creative courage is stoked for the next two months.

- May 26th: New Moon in Gemini - This fertile two-week cycle kickstarts a renaissance in how you share your authentic voice and gifts.

June 2025

Overview Horoscope for the Month:

June brings an electrifying start to your personal renaissance, dear Cancer! The month begins with motivating Mars igniting your passion projects and romantic flair as it tours fiery Leo. This cosmic power injection has you radiating confidence and charisma. Just watch for flare-ups of drama or impatience once Mercury turns retrograde mid-month.

The Full Moon Lunar Eclipse on June 11th precipitates jarring events or startling revelations around your home, family or living situation that demand your full attention. Though potentially disruptive, this lunation is clearing the way for vital changes and rebirths ahead. Trust the bigger picture unfolding.

The solstice on June 20th sees the Sun entering your sign, marking your astrological new year! Set fresh intentions under the potent Cancer New Moon on the 25th. This is an epic time of rebirth, recalibration and remembering who you were born to become.

Love:

Sparks are destined to fly in your love life this June with several astrological hotspots activating your romantic sectors! In the first half, audacious Mars tours Leo, firing up your charisma and sexual magnetism. If coupled, this transit brings a resurgence of passion and playfulness. For singles, your confidence and desirability are running extremely high.

The caveat arrives when communication planet Mercury turns retrograde on June 9th until July 7th. Old relationship dynamics or past lovers could resurface now, requiring you to gain closure before moving forward. Stay self-aware about projecting melodramatic stories onto your partner too. The Lunar Eclipse on the 11th provides radical liberation from whatever has been sabotaging intimacy.

Career:

Your professional life receives an adrenaline boost early in June as lusty Mars travels through your fulfillment sector until the 17th. During this cycle, don't be afraid to assert your talents and capabilities. An unapologetic attitude and aura of charisma and ease will draw promising opportunities your way.

However, do review any important documents carefully after the 9th when messenger Mercury turns retrograde. There may be delays, misunderstandings or

revisions required in contracts, negotiations or creative
projects. After the 22nd, these frustrations should clear
up - but maintain patience in the meantime.

The Cancer New Moon on June 25th marks the
perfect yearly moment for recalibrating your career
goals and updating your personal brand/mission. How
do you most want to shine?

Finances:

With abundant cosmic activity lighting up your
earned income sector, making money is highlighted
this month! Early June could bring exciting new
moneymaking avenues through your charisma, talents
or creative skills as bold Mars blazes through until the
17th. Don't hesitate to showcase what you uniquely
offer.

However, cosmic keystones of financial astrology -
Venus and Mercury - will both be retrograde from June
3rd through July. This could invite money delays,
confusion or temporary cash crunches that require
extra patience and care with spending decisions.
Review documents cautiously and be willing to revise
plans as needed. This retrograde will clear beautifully
for positive forward movement by late July.

Health:

Make caring for your body and overall vitality a top priority this June, dear Cancer! With the first three weeks activating your health and routine sector, you're being cosmically guided to take ownership of any self-care regimens or medical treatments requiring more disciplined follow-through. The results will be worth your consistent efforts!

Keep in mind that messenger Mercury will be reversing through this same area from June 16th through July, so stay open to new information that may prompt course adjustments. If you've been on the fence about trying a new modality or approach, this retrograde is fantastic for researching alternatives. Above all, nourish yourself and trust your body's wisdom.

Travel:

Unexpected travel opportunities could manifest for you from mid-June onward, whether or international voyages or unplanned staycations! With the Lunar Eclipse arriving on the 11th these trips, while potentially chaotic, are meant to awaken you to new realities. Adopt a flexible, open-hearted mindset when journeying so the universe can shower you with delightful surprises.

After the 20th when the Sun shifts into your sign, any trips are highly favored as they'll reconnect you with your truest self and soul's compass. Book spontaneously if you can or take a local excursion somewhere providing freedom and perspective-broadening. Solo adventures work best for getting centered before your big rebirth ahead.

Insights from the Stars:

This June's cosmic wisdom reminds you that rebirth is an ongoing process of spiraling ever closer to your most authentic embodied self-expression. Each year you shed old skins that no longer serve your spirit's evolution and enter fresh cycles of metamorphosis.

The Cancer New Moon on the 25th marks an especially powerful inception point for consciously embracing the core of who you've always been underneath any labels, roles or limiting stories. Emerge fully this month as your spectacular sovereign self without apologies! Let all that makes you uniquely you shine forth brilliantly like a radiant, living work of sacred art.

Best Days in June:

- June 2nd: First Quarter Moon in Virgo - Energy is high for launching a new health, work or organizational regimen.
- June 9th: Mercury Retrograde begins - Temporarily pause on major launches as delays or revisions may be necessary. Great for rest/introspection.
- June 11th: Full Moon/Lunar Eclipse in Sagittarius - Major shakeups and disruptive events occur around home/family. Embrace the necessary transformation.
- June 15th: Jupiter square Saturn - Conflicts in beliefs/philosophies require compromise and expanded perspectives.
- June 20th: Sun enters Cancer - Happy Solstice and astrological new year! A beautiful rebirth commences.
- June 25th: New Moon in Cancer - Make a cosmic wish for your heart's deepest desires! An incredibly fertile cycle for reinvention dawns.

July 2025

Overview Horoscope for the Month:

July marks the heart of your astrological season, providing a fertile window for reinvention and rebirth, dear Cancer. The month begins with Mercury still retrograde until the 7th, so simply allow the first week to complete any unfinished private processing before you launch bold new initiatives. After the 9th, you'll feel increasingly energized to step into the spotlight and shine!

An exciting highlight arrives on the 7th when revolutionary Uranus ingresses into Gemini, your solar house of self-expression, communication and daily routines. For the next seven years, radical awakenings and unexpected liberations will spark across these life areas - just go with the thrilling flow. The New Moon in Leo on July 24th is an ideal launchpad for creative projects synthesizing the old with the new you.

Love:

Your romantic life promises excitement and potential game-changing plot twists in July! The month begins with amorous Venus still backspinning until the 4th, bringing the possibility of reunions or second chances with past lovers. If it's meant to be, it will feel fated - but don't force anything artificial.

From mid-month onward, once love planet Venus enters Leo, passion and charisma are running extremely high. You'll be oozing magnetic radiance and desirous of fun, romance and embodying your sensual self. Just watch for melodrama or control power struggles once Venus opposes rigid Saturn on the 30th. Singles could attract intense attractions that might be karmic initiations worth exploring.

Career:

July's astrology doesn't provide an incredibly auspicious climate for outward-directed ambition, as the cosmos are focused more on your inner processes. However, you'll find inspired motivation for creative pursuits, intellectual or literary projects, and generally allowing your unique self-expression to flow freely.

The career breakthrough you've been waiting for may arrive unexpectedly after Uranus' ingress into Gemini on the 7th radically shifts your daily work patterns, routines and approach to service. Innovative new roles that allow more independence could start rolling in if you stay alert to signals from the universe.

Finances:

Financial themes could require adjustment or recalibration early in July while Mercury is retrograde until the 7th. Rather than pushing ahead with new monetary plans, use this first week to complete outstanding taxes, invoices or budget revisions so your slate is clean after the 9th.

From there, take advantage of several astrological hot spots this month reigniting your money-making magnetism! The New Moon in Leo on the 24th marks the beginning of an incredibly fertile season for manifesting lucrative offers and prosperous opportunities through talents, creativity and authenticity. Have the courage to share your gifts with the world, and the universe will reward you generously.

Health:

With the Sun and New Moon igniting your sign in July, this month provides a powerful window for hitting the reset button on any health matters and self-care routines that feel outdated or stagnant. Take this annual period to assess what is and isn't serving your vitality, then make appropriate adjustments.

Small changes to diet, fitness, rest patterns and the home environment you dwell in can yield significant long-term results. Listen to your body's intuitive guidance and invest time in therapies and modalities that restore your luminous glow from the inside out. A disciplined approach embracing realistic micro-steps is best.

Travel:

July's planetary climate creates an ambient atmosphere supporting casual day trips and impromptu wanderings close to home rather than extended journeys. However, any sojourns near water - beaches, lakes, rivers - are highly favored and could help open you to spontaneous self-realizations, creative downloads and spiritual awakenings.

When Uranus enters Gemini on the 7th, get ready for a turn of unexpected events and opportunities for travel coming your way! Exciting international connections, conference speaking opportunities or learning adventures could start popping up in the coming months through your work and routines. Resolve to stay open-hearted and embrace any opportunities to expand your vision.

Insights from the Stars:

This July's star wisdom reminds you that freedom is an inside job. Any feelings of restlessness, boredom or existential dissatisfaction you're experiencing are your soul's gentle prompts to peel off another illusory layer and express your truth more radically.

With Uranus revolutionizing your self-expression sector from the 7th onward, you're being catalyzed to embrace profound authenticity on an entirely new level. So observe the impulse for change without judging yourself - these are sacred stirrings encouraging you to metamorphose into your highest embodiment. Let inspiration flow through the cracks and surprise yourself by living ever more uninhibited.

Best Days of the Month:

- July 7th: Uranus enters Gemini - A radically awakened new chapter commences around communications, local environments and routines.
- July 13th: Ceres Retrograde in Aries - Reexamine patterns of self-nurturance and boundaries with family.
- July 19th: Jupiter quintile Chiron - Tremendous healing and resolution around core wounds or blocks is possible. Embrace miracles!
- July 24th: New Moon in Leo - The seeds you plant today have incredible gestational

power. Wishes around creativity, fertility and courage bear luxuriant fruit.

- July 30th: Venus opposes Saturn - Commitment issues may feel heightened, but this transit helps separate the wheat from the chaff in relationships.

August 2025

Overview Horoscope for the Month:

August brings thrilling plot twists and unexpected course corrections for you, dear Cancer! The month begins with the skies electrified by July's ingress of radically awakening Uranus into Gemini, governing your daily routines, mindset and immediate surroundings. Disruptions to your usual rhythms should be embraced as cosmic wake-up calls jolting you into greater presence.

The Leo New Moon on July 24th launched you into an extremely fertile season for creative self-expression, romantic possibilities and courageous life reinvention that peaks around the 22nd. Don't shrink from the spotlight - this is your time to shine! Just prepare for intensity when passionate Mars opposes Pluto on the 6th, which could provoke power struggles.

An especially auspicious career opening manifests near the 11th when structured Saturn forms an incredibly stabilizing trine to Uranus. An innovative work opportunity allowing more autonomy may arrive, perfectly synthesizing your evolving values with pragmatic responsibilities.

Love:

Your romantic life is absolutely sizzling throughout August's fiery Leo season! In the first half of the month, red-hot Mars blazes through your partnership sector until the 17th, catalyzing chemistry, attraction and potential power struggles with your significant other or potential paramours. Just know that any relational intensity you're experiencing is forging deeper intimacy if navigated consciously.

From the 17th onward, once audacious Mars enters Virgo, you'll find your libido running very high, with potential for secret attractions or tantalizing flirtations. Coupled Crabs should schedule ample private couple time to thoroughly indulge these erotic stirrings! However you experience the romantic renaissance this month, open yourself to magical reconnection.

Career:

With expansive Jupiter touring your success sector for the past year, opportunities for career growth and achievement have been consistently opening for you. This month, the planet of miracles forms two incredibly auspicious alignments - a trine to Chiron on August 3rd and a fortuitous sextile to Uranus on August 28th. These cosmic boosts illuminate your most authentic, soul-aligned professional path with unusual clarity.

The Saturn-Uranus trine on the 11th could bring an innovative new position, entrepreneurial idea or exciting partnership that allows you more freedom while still providing necessary structure. Be willing to embrace disruption to your usual routines - the shake-ups serve your overall evolution. Finances, responsibilities and creative expression are beautifully synthesized near month's end.

Finances:

August helps you stabilize financial foundations while also encouraging fiscal expansion through creative talents and entrepreneurship. In the first half, prudent Saturn's trine to Uranus could bring an influx of income through digitally-linked businesses or monetization of your unique skills and interests.

After the 23rd, the Sun's entry into Virgo turns your focus towards practical budgeting and rebalancing your net worth. This monthly money review is assisted by grounded, analytical Virgo energy helping you precisely allocate funds as needed while also looking for lucrative new income streams. What innovative earnings concepts can you monetize?

Health:

Your body's health is being cosmically spotlighted in August, providing important revelations and potential course adjustments or beginnings of new regimens. As go-getter Mars tours your wellness sector until the 17th, you'll feel inspired to adopt more vigorous physical routines that push you slightly outside your comfort zone. Just avoid burnout or injury from overexertion.

The New Moon in Virgo on the 23rd marks an ideal two-week phase for establishing new, sustainable lifestyle habits - perhaps an anti-inflammatory meal plan or mobility program to increase flexibility? Work with your body's wisdom and be willing to implement the changes your vitality is requiring. Nurturing self-care yields radiant results!

Travel:

Opportunities for adventure, mind-expanding cultural immersions and exciting getaways abound this month! The first two weeks are perfect for impromptu road trips or weekend excursions close to home but still imbued with spontaneity and magic. An open, playful spirit is the ideal travel mindset now.

From mid-month onward, once Mars enters Virgo, you may feel the call towards more enriching educational or consciousness-expanding voyages.

Learning opportunities through workshops, retreats or intensives could arise unexpectedly - say yes! Broadening your perspectives releases you from limiting mindsets and introduces solutions beyond your previous imaginings.

Insights from the Stars:

This August's star wisdom reveals that your creative courage and self-expression are meant to be this season's headliners! Any inhibitions, plays for validation or attachments to societal approval systems are falling away so you can more freely embody the radiant artist you were born to become.

Paradoxically, it's by choosing to walk your own unconventional path - rocking the traditional career/lifestyle boat and embracing taboo subjects - that you discover your truest power and soul's purpose. Particularly when Uranus opposes the Sun mid-month, you'll feel cosmic prompts to liberate your voice in ways that may startle others but catalyze positive change. Stay spiritually inspired and let inspiration soar!

Best Days of the Month:

- August 3rd: Jupiter trine Chiron - Tremendous healing, teaching and prosperity expands your influence in beautiful ways.
- August 6th: Mars opposes Pluto - Heightened intensity demands radical authenticity and conscious power.
- August 11th: Saturn trine Uranus - An innovative new path/opportunity opens for more autonomy and freedom within structure.
- August 22nd: Mercury enters Libra - Lovely relationship renewals, creative inspiration and poetry flow abundantly.
- August 23rd: New Moon in Virgo - Fertile seeds for upgrading health, work and self-care regimens are planted now.
- August 28th: Jupiter sextile Uranus - Lightning bolt epiphanies and exciting changes arrive related to life philosophies or travel.

September 2025

Overview for the Month:

September is going to be an intense ride for you, Cancer! The first half of the month is turbo-charged by fiery Mars blazing through the area of your chart that rules your daily routines, work, and health. This extra cosmic energy will help motivate you to make some serious positive changes to your lifestyle and habits.

However, things get even more dramatic mid-month as we build up to the potent Virgo New Moon on September 21st, which also features a partial solar eclipse! This super-charged lunation is activating your spirituality sector, giving you a cosmic green light to purge any destructive patterns or negative mental programming that's still holding you back. As unsettling as this process may feel, trust that it's part of your personal rebirth.

The intensity keeps rising after September 22nd when go-getter Mars moves into the relationship area of your chart for the next six weeks. Your closest partnerships and situationships will likely become mirrors, reflecting back to you how courageous (or fear-based) you're being. Radical honesty with yourself and others is required.

Love:

Your love life could get spicy in the first few weeks while passionate Mars tours Virgo! Couples should make plenty of private time to thoroughly explore intimacy and release any pent-up sexual energy – this cosmic energy is meant to be expressed. For singles, you may find yourself attracting exciting new prospects, but look beneath the surface. Are they really seeking connection, or just projecting fantasies?

After mid-month when Mars shifts into Libra, any power struggles or control issues within committed relationships will absolutely come to a head. While these tensions may be uncomfortable, they're helping to reshape your relating patterns for more conscious partnerships. Don't avoid the hard talks – they're necessary for real growth.

Career:

With structured Saturn spending its final weeks in a spiritual sector of your chart, you may find yourself questioning your core dreams and beliefs about your greater purpose. September's intensity could feel profoundly unsettling at times as you let go of any outdated or limited visions that no longer resonate.

The Virgo Solar Eclipse on September 21st marks a powerful reboot for your daily work, services to others, and overall physical vitality. From this point forward, your tasks and output gain deeper meaning when linked to some higher mission. Though delays or changes may be frustrating now, the detours are ultimately adjusting your trajectory to your most impactful role. Stay open!

Finances:

September's cosmic commotion will likely bring some financial shake-ups that require you to be flexible and responsive. In the beginning of the month while Saturn is still touring Pisces, focus on reviewing any debts, investments or long-term savings strategies. Listen to your intuition over just numbers on a spreadsheet.

From September 3rd onward, the karmic North Node shifts into steady Taurus, helping you stabilize your foundations like home and income-generating assets. Patience and consistent effort yield rewards now. The end of September is an especially fertile time for manifesting lucrative business breakthroughs if you're willing to take calculated risks aligned with your higher purpose.

Health:

With fiery Mars charging through the health and routine area of your chart for the first three weeks, you'll likely feel extra motivated to adopt some new exercise, diet or self-care program that challenges you in a good way. Pick one goal that feels sustainable and pour your energy into it!

The Virgo New Moon Eclipse on September 21st kicks off a powerful new cycle for upgrading your preventative wellness practices from a holistic mind-body-spirit approach. If you've been dealing with any chronic issues, this is the time to explore complementary therapies or look at root causes. Be patient and trust that any lifestyle upgrades begun now will have long-lasting benefits.

Travel:

With go-getter Mars firing up the domestic area of your chart until September 22nd, you may feel more inspired to stick close to home this month and get productive around the house. However, any impromptu regional trips that do come up around the 21st's eclipse could bring some unexpected shakeups or detours involving friends and family. Stay flexible!

After Mars moves into your partnership sector on the 22nd, an adventurous vacation with your spouse or closest friend could be exactly what you need to help expand your perspectives. Being immersed in unfamiliar environments centered around consciousness-expanding experiences or relationships is ideal. Remember, any travel for you right now is helping you transcend limited self-beliefs, so stay open!

Insights from the Stars:

The key cosmic lesson this September is about awakening through the purging process, dear Cancer. The universe is sending some major wake-up calls designed to help shed old layers of self-deception, limiting beliefs, and fears around intimacy, purpose and authentic self-expression. While this stripping phase may feel chaotic and unsettling, try to view it from a higher lens of ultimate liberation.

The more you can embrace the dissolution and "liquefying" of your old stuck identities, the more brilliantly your true radiant essence can shine forth. Call on your bravery when the cosmos gets rocky – your personal rebirth is both necessary and inevitable. You're becoming free on the deepest soul levels.

Best Days:

- Sept 3rd - True Node enters Taurus, kicking off an 18-month cycle for stabilizing your values and self-worth.
- Sept 7th - Lunar Eclipse ushering in releases around your daily work, service, or health routines. Embrace change.
- Sept 17th - Mars trine Pluto gives you incredible willpower and courage to pursue your heart's desires.
- Sept 21st - Virgo New Moon/Solar Eclipse initiating a fertile new cycle for remaking your vitality and identity.
- Sept 23rd - When Mercury enters Libra, communication and social connections will start flowing more harmoniously.
- Sept 29th - Mars trine Saturn helps you take calculated risks and make bold new commitments that change the game.

October 2025

Overview for the Month:

Buckle up, Cancer, because October is going to be an intense, transformational ride! The month kicks off with go-getter Mars still blazing through the relationship area of your chart, forming a fiery square to intense Pluto on the 4th. Any toxic power dynamics or deep-rooted issues in your closest partnerships will absolutely demand to be dealt with - no more bypassing or avoiding.

However, your ability to embrace rebirth and reinvent yourself gets majorly amplified after October 24th when taskmaster Saturn moves into Aries and the most personal sector of your chart. For the next 2.5 years, this planet is going to be stripping away anything inauthentic so that your most resilient, true self can finally emerge. While this process will inevitably feel unsettling at times, trust that it's restructuring you for an incredible evolution.

Emotional breakdowns are likely around the 26th when love planet Venus opposites shocking Uranus, shaking up your relationships and finances. But these destabilizing events are ultimately paving the way for the Scorpio New Moon Ecplise on October 27th to initiate a brand new 6-month cycle of profound personal rebirth and transformation. Get ready!

Love:

The romantic tensions keep rising throughout October while fiery Mars battles it out with powerful Pluto (4th) and then forms a challenging square to structure planet Saturn (23rd). If there's any unfinished baggage, manipulation games or control issues playing out in your closest partnerships, they're going to reach a breaking point now. You'll have to decide whether to make soul-level, permanent changes or consciously walk away.

That said, a surprising breath of fresh air arrives mid-month when Mars links up with revolutionary Uranus on the 17th, potentially introducing exciting new relationship prospects or alternative relating models you could explore. Stay open-minded and non-judgmental about whatever excites your spirit! Just watch for disruptive plot twists and breakdowns around month's end when Venus clashes with Uranus - these are ultimately catalyzing positive growth.

Career:

October kicks off a profoundly pivotal 2.5-year career cycle with structured Saturn's ingress into Aries and your identity sector on the 24th. For the next few years, this planet will be overhauling your self-concept and dismantling any professional paths, goals or work that's misaligned with your soul's truth. While feeling disoriented at times is inevitable, these mini-destructions create space for rebuilding a fully authentic vocation.

Luckily, the Scorpio New Moon Solar Eclipse on the 27th marks the start of a fertile new 6-month cycle of reinvention linked to your self-worth, income streams and confidence in sharing your unique gifts. As layers of outdated identities peel away, you'll start attracting career opportunities that are a true soul-level match. Follow any unconventional callings now without self-doubt.

Finances:

You'll receive more than one wake-up call around money matters this October, requiring you to stabilize your foundations but also embrace innovative income streams that feel spiritually-aligned. First, on the 17th, prosperous Jupiter clashes intensely with transformative Pluto, amplifying the consequences of any overspending, debt accumulation or financial recklessness.

However, abundance breakthroughs are very possible when the karmic North Node aligns with Jupiter later in the month, showering you with blessings and prosperity through your social networks or community engagement. Just steer clear of any risky money moves around the 26th's Venus-Uranus clash, which could bring some chaotic cash crunches. Be patient - the bigger picture is unfolding positively.

Health:

With powerhouse Saturn entering one of the health zones in your chart on October 24th, tuning into your body's needs and establishing consistent self-care rituals becomes an absolute cosmic priority for the next 2.5 years. Any unhealthy imbalances or lifestyle ruts you've been in will inevitably be destabilized now, pushing you to get proactive through positive new routines, treatments or modalities.

The Scorpio Solar Eclipse on the 27th clears the way for an especially fertile mind-body rebirth cycle to begin in November/December. This lunation is nudging you to approach your vitality from a holistic perspective, exploring modalities that honor the whole human being rather than just symptoms. Consider reviving some ancient or ancestral wisdom about natural living too.

Travel:

Expect the unexpected when it comes to travel this October! Any trips that do manifest - whether planned in advance or highly spontaneous - are absolutely guaranteed to shake up your perspectives and deliver eye-opening revelations that catapult your personal growth.

Your craving for adventure and mind-expanding journeys intensifies from mid-month onward once Mars links up with revolutionary Uranus on the 17th. Whether it's an off-the-beaten-track bucket list destination, a rustic retreat or consciousness-centered intensive, being immersed in new cultural scenery will powerfully inspire you on many levels. Don't hesitate to pack your bags and go wherever calls you boldly!

Insights from the stars:

The big cosmic lesson radiating through the stars this October centers around authenticity and self-actualization being the keys to your ultimate freedom and liberation, dear Crab. Over these next few years, Saturn's influence in your identity sector will inevitably cause any self-limiting identities, values or paths that don't resonate with your soul's truth to shatter and collapse.

While these seeds of ego-dissolution may feel incredibly disruptive across your personal or professional life, it's vital to zoom out and view everything through a higher lens of spiritual awakening. You're being divinely broken down so that you can fully rebirth into the most luminous version of your authentic self. Summon your courage through the chaos, stay spiritually inspired, and prepare yourself to radically embody who you were born to become!

Best Days of the Month:
- October 4th - Mars-Pluto square reigniting intensity around intimacy, boundaries and power dynamics demanding change.
- October 13th - Aries Full Moon marking a culmination or revelation around identities, independence and life direction.
- October 17th - Jupiter-Pluto square and Mars-Uranus trine presenting game-changing opportunities for reinvention/expansion if you take calculated risks.
- October 24th - Saturn's powerful ingress into Aries kicks off a 2.5-year cycle overhauling your purpose, identity and lifecourse.

- October 27th - Scorpio New Moon/Solar Eclipse catalyzing a 6-month rebirth process linked to your confidence and ability to monetize your unique gifts and talents.

November 2025

Overview for the Month:

November promises to be a pivotal month of profound inner shift and outer restructuring for you, Cancer. The intensity from October's eclipses and planetary ingresses continues building, ultimately culminating in a cosmic reckoning of sorts by month's end. Stay centered and trust that these turbulence are serving your greater awakening and evolution.

The first three weeks bring a slowed, introspective pace as messenger Mercury turns retrograde on November 9th. Use this signal scrambler for productive rest, reflection and tying up any loose ends. By the 20th, you'll feel immense motivation returning for manifesting positive changes on the material plane.

An especially accelerated period arrives on November 27th when warrior planet Mars forms an electrifying alignment with engineering Saturn. This cosmic power couple inspires you to take calculated risks and make bold commitments aligned with your soul's truth. Monumental transformation and quantum leaps are absolutely inevitable now!

Love:

Your love life is likely to be a source of significant growth and possible turbulence this November. If in an existing partnership, simmering tensions, resentments or control dynamics that have been brewing could reach a breaking point during the first half of the month as Mercury revisits this area of your chart. Have courage to confront lingering issues once and for all - true vulnerability and transparency are required for lasting change.

If single, your romantic resilience may feel tested as the month unfolds. However, by November's final weeks, a profound clarity and inner resetting emerges that magnetizes your future soulmate or conscious collaborators. You're evolving beyond any prior relating limitations now.

Career:

With Mercury backspinning until November 29th, this isn't an ideal cycle for outward-directed ambition, big launches or self-promotion - at least not until the second half of December after the retrograde dust settles. In the meantime, use this sleepy professional time for introspection, reassessment and tying up any loose administrative ends.

However, a hugely promising new direction begins illuminating for you around November 27th's potent Mars-Saturn alignment, which highlights hidden opportunities in your career and sense of purpose. An innovative self-employment role, leadership position or entrepreneurial collaboration could manifest, finally synthesizing your kaleidoscope of talents and spiritual beliefs into an authentic, lucrative role.

Finances:

November's planetary skies bring some turbulence and restructuring to your financial foundations, requiring patience and trust in the bigger picture unfolding. The first half of the month sees Mercury reversing through the money zones of your chart, potentially creating cash flow squeezes, payment delays or adjustments required to budgets and investments. Avoid major purchases if possible until after December 9th when the retrograde concludes.

Around the 7th, your prosperity could receive a welcome boost through expanded social networks, publishing opportunities or possibly an inheritance. Just be cautious with any risky ventures around the Lunar Eclipse on November 19th, as hidden financial vulnerabilities may suddenly be exposed within a business or partnership.

Health:

Your physical vitality becomes replenished this November after several months of potential depletion or burnout. The first three weeks of the month are ideal for engaging in self-care practices, establishing sustainable exercise routines and easing back into wellness regimes. With Mercury retrograde through this sector until Thanksgiving, you may need to research alternative therapies or mindset shifts to support your holistic well-being.

After the 20th, you'll feel an undeniable surge in vigor and motivation to implement positive lifestyle upgrades, new diets or workout programs. An auspicious healing window opens in early December, so be patient about making any major health overhauls now - simply set the philosophical foundation and establish productive daily habits.

Travel:

The cosmic winds are not particularly favoring adventurous journeys or exploration in November, dear Crab. The first three weeks see Mercury reversing through the wanderlust zone of your chart, increasing the potential for miscommunications, delays and general chaos when traveling - you may need to reschedule any trips planned for this cycle.

However, the end of November ushers in an electrifying Mars-Saturn alignment that could deliver unexpected opportunities for travel connected to business or entrepreneurial themes in early 2023. Remain open to attending conferences, educational retreats or other "working vacations" that expose you to expansive personal and professional growth. This window is about expanding your vision of what is truly possible.

Insights from the Stars:

The key cosmic insight radiating through November's stars reveals the profound inner metamorphosis occurring within you, Cancer. Any stubborn self-limiting beliefs, fears or outdated attachments obstructing your path will absolutely reach a breaking point under this month's astrological heat, forcing you to transmute them into higher states of consciousness.

Rather than clinging to stories of victimhood, you're being spiritually awakened to recognize your own divine power to reshape reality through focused intention, thoughts and emotions. As chaotic as November's intensities may feel, try to align with the unstoppable, self-sovereignty emerging within your soul! The universe is conspiring to liberate you into your full authentic potency.

Best Days of the Month:

- November 7th: North Node aligns with Jupiter - opportunities for income growth and expansion through social networks, education or publishing.
- November 9th: Mercury Retrograde begins - delays, revisions and miscommunications around career, routine and self-care become activated. Rest and reflect.
- November 19th: Full Moon Lunar Eclipse - exposing hidden financial vulnerabilities or imbalances within a business/partnership. Adjust accordingly.
- November 20th: Sun enters Sagittarius - Your vital energies receive a welcome boost after last month's potential depletion.
- November 27th: Mars-Saturn alignment - An electrifying catalyst for calculated risk-taking and making bold, life-restructuring commitments aligned with your highest truth.

December 2025

Overview for the Month:

The year is winding down but the intensity certainly isn't letting up for you this December, Cancer! The first three weeks bring a welcome slowdown, helping you catch your breath after last month's cosmic chaos and intensity. Use this grounding period to reflect, rest and realign before an incredibly fertile new annual cycle kicks off around the 21st.

You'll start to feel your vital life force returning as the Sun enters Capricorn on the 21st, aligning with the Solstice and activating your personal rebirth. The New Moon in Capricorn two days later marks an extraordinary window for resetting intentions and planting seeds for manifestation in 2026. Give yourself permission to boldly dream into the grandest visions for your becoming!

While the holidays could stir up some sentimental visitors from your past, maintain your center as you approach this threshold initiation. You're being divinely guided to shed any remaining limiting attachments so you can finally emerge as the fully empowered sovereign you were born to become.

Love:

Your romantic connections and partnerships continue undergoing major transformations in December, as the month's astrology contains both significant blessings and potential disruptions. If in a committed relationship, challenges that surfaced in November could reach a make-or-break climax early in the month. Have courage to either recommit on an entirely new level of intimacy, truth and transparency, or lovingly part ways.

For singles, December could see you attracting thrilling new amours and flirtations, but be discerning about motivations. Is this potential suitor aligned with your values and evolution? Pleasure-seeking connections without depth may disappoint. Your resilience will be tested to see how grounded you are in self-love.

By the Solstice on the 21st, an attitude of romantic renewal and passion blossoms! Singles will magnetize soulmate connections attuned to their rebirth, while couples experience psychic rejoining through vulnerability and mutual surrender. Follow the currents of love consciously unfolding.

Career:

After November's potential stagnation or uncertainties in your professional life, December delivers a breath of revitalizing fresh air for manifesting breakthroughs! The first three weeks are perfect for resting and resetting so you can clarify your vision. Then from the 21st onward, you'll feel unstoppable motivation and enthusiasm.

The New Moon on the 23rd marks an ideal time to take action steps towards manifesting an authentic vocation in alignment with your reawakened passion and soul's purpose. Any innovative entrepreneurial ideas, indie creative projects or leadership roles helping uplift humanity are destined to thrive. Focus on demonstrating your unique value and gifts.

However, you could also encounter obstructive egos or power struggles with colleagues or partners this month who aren't aligned with your mission. Stay impeccable in your integrity and witness jealousy or dismissiveness with compassion. Rise above any naysayers.

Finances:

The financial sectors of your chart receive multiple cosmic boosts this December that could yield exciting windfalls or income surges in 2026. However, you'll first need to get a bit more rigorous about examining your financial foundations and making adjustments early in the month.

Around the 7th, review any blind spots in your budgets, investments or revenue streams. With structured Saturn touring your money zone for the next few years, building sustainable practices around earning and allocating your resources is required for growth. Cosmic helpers like the Capricorn New Moon on the 23rd magnetize powerful opportunities to monetize your offerings and talents. Invest in your worth!

Health:

Your physical vitality makes a strong resurgence throughout December after any potential depletion or imbalances late last year. The first three weeks provide a sweet spot for resting, turning within and attuning to your body's wisdom without outer pressures. Take some rejuvenating solo time in nature to decompress and recenter.

After the 21st, you'll feel powerfully motivated to upgrade lifestyle habits and daily routines around diet, fitness, sleep and stress management. The New Moon on the 23rd launches an especially fertile new cycle for embracing mind-body modalities that honor your holistic wellbeing. What new rituals feel energetically aligned?

Travel:

With go-getter Mars touring the wanderlust sector of your chart from mid-month onward, you'll likely feel an inexorable pull to seek scenery and environments beyond your usual stomping grounds. This cosmic helper provides tremendous courage, momentum and virility for epic adventures to destinations that help expand your perspectives!

Use the slower first three weeks to plan out any bucket list journeys you're feeling inspired to embark upon in 2026. Whether an international pilgrimage, conscious retreat or exploration of sacred sites closer to home - you're being divinely guided to step outside your comfort zones. Where is your soul calling you to explore? Book those flights!

Insights from the Stars:

The key celestial insight woven through December's skies is one of profound individual empowerment and sovereignty through self-trust. Any lingering attachments to disempowering narratives, limiting beliefs, or approval seeking from external sources is cosmic completion -you're outgrowing the old entirely.

As the calendar year draws to a close, you're experiencing an extraordinary soul-level rebirth and the births of an entirely new relating to yourself, your purpose and untamed authenticity. Your words, presence, and quality of love you radiate are destined to move worlds if you simply surrender attachments to the known and remain open to the surprising awe your future holds. Trust your process. Magic is upon you.

Best Days of the Month:

- December 3rd: Gemini Full Moon - Epiphanies and possible reunions around communications, mindset or local communities. Revelations abound.
- December 7th: Mercury Direct - The cosmic messenger finally goes direct after an extended retrograde period, clearing the path forward. Review your budgets/investments.
- December 14th: Venus enters Aquarius - Your social connections and networks become activated for positive synchronicity and expansion. Say "yes!"
- December 21st: Sun enters Capricorn/Solstice - The start of an incredibly auspicious new annual cycle for you. Rebirth is initiated!

- December 23rd: New Moon in Capricorn - This is your cosmic launchpad for planting seeds of new intentions and embodying your grandest, most authentic visions for 2026.

Made in the USA
Las Vegas, NV
16 December 2024

14457388R00066